Novels for Students, Volume 31

Project Editor: Sara Constantakis Rights Acquisition and Management: Jennifer Altschul, Margaret Chamberlain-Gaston, Leitha Etheridge-Sims, Kelly Quin Composition: Evi Abou-El-Seoud Manufacturing: Drew Kalasky

Imaging: John Watkins

Product Design: Pamela A. E. Galbreath, Jennifer Wahi Content Conversion: Katrina Coach Product Manager: Meggin Condino © 2010 Gale, Cengage Learning

For product information and technology assistance, contact us at **Gale Customer Support, 1-800-877-4253.**

For permission to use material from this text or product, submit all requests online at **www.cengage.com/permissions.**

Further permissions questions can be emailed to **permissionrequest@cengage.com** While every effort has been made to ensure the reliability of the information presented in this publication, Gale, a part of Cengage Learning, does not guarantee the accuracy of the data contained herein. Gale accepts no payment for listing; and inclusion in the publication of any organization, agency, institution, publication, service, or individual does not imply endorsement of the editors or publisher. Errors brought to the attention of the publisher and verified to the satisfaction of the publisher will be corrected in future editions.

Gale
27500 Drake Rd.
Farmington Hills, MI, 48331-3535

ISBN-13: 978-1-4144-4169-6
ISBN-10: 1-4144-4169-X
ISSN 1094-3552

This title is also available as an e-book.
ISBN-13: 978-1-4144-4947-0

ISBN-10: 1-4144-4947-X

Contact your Gale, a part of Cengage Learning sales
representative for ordering information.

Printed in the United States of America
1 2 3 4 5 6 7 14 13 12 11 10

Zen and the Art of Motorcycle Maintenance

Robert Pirsig 1974

Introduction

Robert Pirsig's *Zen and the Art of Motorcycle Maintenance: An Inquiry into Values* is a novel, often described as semi-autobiographical, narrated in the first person (the narrator refers to himself as "I") by an unnamed man. The story he tells is described as a series of "Chautauquas." (A Chautauqua, in brief, is a series of stories or lectures intended to educate and entertain.) The narrator's story is a divided one, in part concerned with a cross-country motorcycle trip he is taking from

Minnesota to California with his young son and a couple of friends. It is also the story of the narrator's former personality, whom the narrator identifies by the name of Phaedrus. In the course of describing his current journey, the narrator relates Phaedrus's journey toward insanity and eventual annihilation. Along the way, Phaedrus's ideas regarding the philosophical notion of "Quality" are explained, dissected, and elaborated upon by the narrator. The narrator claims that the purpose of the trip and his analysis of Phaedrus and Phaedrus's worldview is to finally bury Phaedrus properly. Through the course of the novel, however, it is revealed that the personality of Phaedrus, the personality the narrator presumes has been eliminated by the shock-therapy treatment he received in a mental facility, has not, in fact, been destroyed. Phaedrus still resides within the narrator's mind and, furthermore, is attempting to reestablish himself.

Found in both fiction and nonfiction sections of libraries and bookstores, *Zen and the Art of Motorcycle Maintenance*, originally published in 1974, is available in these more recent editions: the twenty-fifth anniversary edition, published in 1999 by First Quill and by Perennial Classics in 2000, and a 2008 edition published by Harper Perennial Modern Classics.

Author Biography

Pirsig, the son of a professor, was born on September 6, 1928, in Minneapolis, Minnesota. Many of the facts regarding Pirsig's life are comparable to the personal history of his narrator in *Zen and the Art of Motorcycle Maintenance*; this has led to the novel being described as a fictionalized autobiography. Like the narrator, Pirsig, as a child, was a gifted student with an IQ of 170 at the age of nine. He began a course of study at the University of Minnesota in 1943 and was expelled two years later due to academic failure. In 1946, Pirsig enlisted in the army and served until 1948. His years of service included serving in Korea for some time.

After returning to the United States, Pirsig re-enrolled at the University of Minnesota, studied chemistry and philosophy, and earned a bachelor of arts degree in 1950. With the help of a tutor, Pirsig was granted a place at Benares Hindu University in India, where he studied Eastern philosophy. After his return, he married Nancy Ann James in 1954. The couple had two children, Christopher and Theodore. Pirsig earned his master of arts degree in journalism from the University of Minnesota in 1958.

Pirsig taught as an instructor of English composition at Montana State College (now University) from 1959 to 1961, where he renewed his interest in philosophy. His focus on a metaphysical notion of quality became single-minded. During this time, Pirsig battled severe anxiety and depression. He pursued graduate studies at the University of Illinois, Chicago, and also taught there as an instructor in rhetoric from 1961 to 1962. During these years, Pirsig's internal struggles intensified. In interviews he has described his particular experience of sitting on the floor of his apartment for days, unmoving, alternately as enlightenment and as catatonic schizophrenia. (Schizophrenia is a severe mental disorder in which the patient has the following symptoms: loss of contact with environment, deteriorating ability to function, delusions, and hallucinations.) He was eventually committed by the court to a mental institution, where he was diagnosed with schizophrenia and received shock therapy (the administering of high-voltage alternating current through his brain). From 1961 to 1963, Pirsig spent time in and out of mental hospitals. He discontinued his treatment in 1964 and found employment as a technical writer.

The motorcycle trip described in *Zen and the Art of Motorcycle Maintenance* took place in 1968. Pirsig's manuscript was rejected over one hundred times, as Pirsig discusses in his afterward to the twenty-fifth anniversary of the novel, but it was finally published in 1974. Pirsig and his first wife divorced in 1978, and he was remarried later that year to Wendy L. Kimball, with whom he had a daughter, Nell. In the year following his second marriage, Pirsig's son Christopher was killed in a violent mugging. Pirsig wrote a sequel to *Zen and the Art of Motorcycle Maintenance* titled *Lila: An Inquiry Into Morals* (1991), in which his "metaphysics of quality" is further explored.

Plot Summary

Part One

CHAPTER ONE

Zen and the Art of Motorcycle Maintenance opens with the narrator riding his motorcycle through the Central Plains. His thoughts are interwoven with his conversation with his young son, Chris, who is on the motorcycle with him. The narrator explains his intention to use the westward journey from their home in Minnesota as an opportunity to discuss some of the things on his mind, and he envisions this experience as a series of "Chautauquas," or a series of lectures intended to entertain and educate. Traveling with the narrator and his son are family friends John and Sylvia Southerland. The narrator explores John's dislike of motorcycle maintenance as an example of a certain "disharmony" that plagues not just John but many people. He describes it as a split between those who value and embrace technology and those who approach life in a more romantic, intuitive manner. John and the narrator's attitudes toward motorcycle maintenance, the narrator explains, shed light on this split and are used to explore the larger implications of the split between rationality and romanticism. The narrator's philosophic approach to such issues in the first chapter sets the tone for the rest of the book.

CHAPTER TWO

The trip and the Chautauqua continue as the narrator observes the subtle change in the country they are riding through, a transition from the Central Plains to the Great Plains. The narrator offers further ruminations on the way motorcycle maintenance and one's attitudes toward it reflect larger issues within society as a whole.

Media Adaptations

- *Zen and the Art of Motorcycle Maintenance: An Inquiry Into Values* was recorded as an unabridged audio CD, read by Michael Kramer and published by Macmillan Audio, 2006.

CHAPTER THREE

The four cyclists (the narrator and his son Chris on one cycle, John and Sylvia on another) have ridden through the Red River Valley and are heading into an approaching storm. As the rain and thunder hit, the narrator has a flash of recognition. When various features of the landscape are illuminated he thinks, "He's *been* here!" This is one of the first clues the narrator offers regarding the alternate personality that has resided within him. The narrator becomes extremely cautious about proceeding in the bad weather, but his conversation with his son suggests that his cautiousness and trepidation are also a response to the resurgence of the other personality. Later, at the hotel where the four are staying, talk turns to ghosts. The narrator's mysterious comments about having known someone who chased a ghost, beat it, and then became a ghost himself foreshadow his later explanations of his relationship with his alternate personality.

CHAPTER FOUR

The narrator offers an extensive list and discussion of the items he has taken with him on this motorcycle trip. The four cyclists ride out of town early—at the urging of the narrator—on a cold morning. John, Sylvia, and Chris are angry with the narrator when they finally stop for breakfast. The mood shifts before they ride again.

CHAPTER FIVE

The riders approach the High Plains and stop in Hague, North Dakota, to plan their route across the Missouri River. The narrator recalls previous conversations with John about motorcycle maintenance and continues to contemplate John's negative reaction to the idea of a person learning the technical and intuitive details of maintaining one's own machine. In an attempt to account for John's attitudes, the narrator observes that there are two distinct realities that people perceive, "one of immediate artistic appearance and of underlying scientific explanation." The narrator observes how these two realities do not seem to fit together very well. After a brief stop, the cyclists continue on to the town of Lemmon. They are all fatigued, but Chris is excited about camping. They find a spot but have difficulties getting set up and preparing dinner. When Chris stalks off after complaining of stomach pains, John, Sylvia, and the narrator discuss his ailment. The narrator explains that Chris's stomach complaint is a recurring one for which they have found no medical explanation. Doctors have told the narrator and his wife that the issue is likely a symptom of mental illness. The narrator tries to explain why he stopped Chris's psychiatric treatments, but he falters, acknowledging only that it did not feel right. After Chris returns and the group falls asleep, the narrator dreams of a figure he describes as evil and insane. He identifies this figure as Phaedrus.

CHAPTER SIX

The narrator decides to discuss Phaedrus, claiming that to omit him from the story would be like running from him. He asserts that Phaedrus was never properly buried, and assumes that is why he, the narrator, feels troubled by the renewed sense of Phaedrus's presence. The cyclists load their gear and head out into the hot day. Prefacing his comments with the statement that Phaedrus will not be praised but buried permanently, the narrator begins to flesh out Phaedrus's theories. Here he further explains ideas he alluded to earlier and discusses at length two modes of human understanding: classical and romantic. Much is made of the division between these two ways of perceiving the world. After commenting on the depths to which Phaedrus probed these ideas, the narrator informs us of Phaedrus's ultimate fate: a police arrest ordered by the court and removal from society. The narrator's thoughts are interrupted by periodic breaks in their journey for coffee and food. He continues to analyze Phaedrus's analytic approach to the classic/romantic split.

CHAPTER SEVEN

The narrator observes the oppressive heat in which they are riding. As the review of Phaedrus's analysis continues, the narrator stresses that Phaedrus was looking for a solution to the classic/romantic divide, a way to unite these two modes of understanding. He sought a theory that would explain and synthesize rather than dissemble and divide. The group passes into Montana, and the narrator explains that the ghost he spoke with Chris about was the "ghost of rationality" that Phaedrus pursued. As the oppressively hot day continues, the narrator rides more slowly to avoid overheating the motorcycle or blowing tires, but John and Sylvia are irritated with his slow pace. He thinks of the way Phaedrus's wife and family suffered due to his inattention. Interspersed with discussions of Phaedrus's thoughts—ideas the narrator claims to have discovered through Phaedrus's writings—are the narrator's recollections of having woken up in a hospital where it was eventually explained to him that he now had a new personality. The narrator further explains that Phaedrus, his former personality, was dead, after the court had ordered him institutionalized and he had undergone shock therapy (the administering of high-voltage alternating current through his brain). He speaks of the fear he feels now, of how he never knew Phaedrus, but everything he sees, he sees with his own eyes, as well as with Phaedrus's. After the slow, hot ride, a cooling rain refreshes the group.

Part Two

CHAPTER EIGHT

Sylvia, John, Chris, and the narrator are in Miles City, Montana. They have slept and bathed and the mood is good. The narrator applies his analysis of the classic/romantic divide to his current maintenance of his cycle. The group discusses their upcoming destination of Bozeman, Montana. As John discusses radical professors from the college in Bozeman, the narrator notes that he has been among them, observing silently that it was Phaedrus, not him, who was one of the professors under discussion. This observation highlights the peculiarities of the narrator's identity: he views himself as a different person entirely from the person he used to be (Phaedrus), but to all outward appearances he seems to be the same person.

CHAPTER NINE

Following the Yellowstone Valley, the group traverses Montana on their way to Bozeman. The narrator's Chautauqua for the day focuses on logic and its uses. He extensively discusses inductive and deductive reasoning.

CHAPTER TEN

The narrator notes that Phaedrus's break from mainstream rational thought can now be discussed. He outlines Phaedrus's thoughts regarding the formation of scientific hypotheses. Phaedrus's analysis led him always to more questions, to pondering the nature of truth. He reveals that Phaedrus, who entered college at the age of fifteen, was expelled by the age of seventeen for failing grades. He was unable to thrive in the academic community when he questioned the basic structures and models of what he was being taught. The narrator notes that Phaedrus at this point began to drift. The group arrives at Laurel, Montana, with the mountains in sight.

CHAPTER ELEVEN

Everyone seems excited and energized by the mountain air. They discuss their path to Bozeman, and they select a route that the narrator recalls Phaedrus having used a number of times. During the next phase of the trip, the narrator explores the truths Phaedrus sought after he left college. He notes that Phaedrus joined the Army and served in Korea and became interested in Eastern philosophy. After his return, Phaedrus renewed his studies at the university in Minnesota, from which he had previously been expelled, focusing on philosophy. As the cyclists travel further into the mountains, the narrator discusses Phaedrus's philosophical journey, commenting on Phaedrus's study of philosophers such as Immanuel Kant and David Hume.

CHAPTER TWELVE

The group is conversing about the person they will be staying with, a former colleague of the narrator. Some anxiety is felt by all, as everyone realizes that the man, an art professor by the name of DeWeese, knew the narrator only as Phaedrus. Though the narrator remembers very little of DeWeese, a few conversations Phaedrus and DeWeese shared come back to him on their way to DeWeese's house. He also explains that between Phaedrus's undergraduate studies and his teaching stint in Bozeman, he spent some time living in India and studying Eastern philosophy at the Benares Hindu University. Following Phaedrus's return to the Midwest, he got a degree in journalism, married, and had two children, and worked as a technical writer. He had, the narrator observes, "given up."

CHAPTER THIRTEEN

The narrator notices how anxious he feels about being back in Bozeman, and recalls

Phaedrus's extreme anxiety about teaching. Further recollections regarding Phaedrus's interest in protecting the college's accreditation requirements are related. For some colleagues it was a political issue, but for Phaedrus it was about the quality of the education the students were receiving.

CHAPTER FOURTEEN

The four travelers enter Bozeman, stop and eat, and then proceed to DeWeese's house where they are greeted by DeWeese and his wife. The narrator is aware that DeWeese still views him as Phaedrus. That evening, Chris tells his father that the previous evening, his father told him that it was lonely here. The narrator has no recollection of the conversation, and assumes Chris was dreaming. After dinner, other guests arrive, Jack and Wylla Barsness. Conversation turns to some of the same topics the narrator has been ruminating about, and he offers a brief lecture on the schism between art and technology.

CHAPTER FIFTEEN

Following some leisure time exploring a mining town, John and Sylvia decide to head back toward Minnesota. Chris and his father will hike into the mountains near Bozeman, then return for the motorcycle to continue their journey. The narrator and Chris walk to the school where Phaedrus used to teach. When the narrator decides to explore one of the buildings, the one containing his former classroom and office, Chris feels scared and runs outside. The narrator proceeds and is overcome with memories. He has the sensation that Phaedrus is present, not as a fragmented part of himself but seeing everything he himself sees. Having returned to the place where his obsession with the metaphysical notion of "Quality" began, the narrator is once again immersed in his former thought processes on the subject.

Part Three

CHAPTER SIXTEEN

Chris and his father begin their journey into the mountains. As they hike, the narrator explores Phaedrus's examination of the notion of Quality. He points out that he is not aware of everything that existed in Phaedrus's mind during this phase of his life, and is now attempting to piece together the remnants he has found. Interspersed with this extensive recollection of his classroom teachings are snippets of conversations with Chris, who appears to be struggling with the arduous hike.

CHAPTER SEVENTEEN

The narrator attempts to encourage Chris, who has grown increasingly frustrated. As their hike continues, the narrator returns to Phaedrus's classroom and his attempts to define and identify Quality. Chris's hiking efforts are defiant and angry.

CHAPTER EIGHTEEN

Phaedrus's quest toward understanding Quality progresses, the narrator informs us, when Phaedrus begins to view Quality as something undefinable. The benefits and pitfalls of this approach are reviewed, and along the way, the narrator continues to urge on his son, who stumbles up the mountain, falls often, and becomes ever more discouraged and angry. They camp for the night.

CHAPTER NINETEEN

Waking, the narrator recalls a dream, one that will recur throughout the rest of the novel in various versions, in which he is separated from Chris, Chris's brother, and mother by a glass door. Chris beckons his father to open the door, but he does not. When the narrator speaks with Chris, Chris tells him that he, the narrator, kept Chris up all night talking about the mountain, and how he would meet Chris at the top. The narrator recalls nothing of this conversation. Once they are on the move again, the narrator returns to his Chautauqua, recalling Phaedrus's tackling of the question of whether or not Quality is subjective. The narrator reveals that Phaedrus began to view Quality as an event, the cause of subjects and objects. This represents a major breakthrough in Phaedrus's theories. Just then, Chris sees blue sky, and realizes they are near the top of the mountain.

CHAPTER TWENTY

Chris is in good spirits, as they have nearly reached the summit of the peak. They discuss Chris's claim that the narrator spoke to him about meeting him at the top of the mountain, and Chris suggests that the narrator sounded like he used to.

The descent down the mountain begins, and the narrator declares that it is time to leave Phaedrus's path and explore some of his own ideas, paths that Phaedrus neglected. The narrator points out that for Phaedrus, the metaphysics of Quality were not channeled into everyday life. Rather, his approach focused on the moment of "nonintellectual awareness," the moment between the "instant of vision" and the "instant of awareness." Phaedrus was increasingly drawn to that in-between moment, when Quality is experienced but not intellectualized, a process which degrades the actual truth of the moment. This awareness, and his being able to link his view with that explored in the Eastern philosophy of the *Tao Te Ching* caused a "slippage" in Phaedrus's mind, a disconnection, the narrator explains.

CHAPTER TWENTY-ONE

Chris and his father struggle through thick brush on their way down the mountain. The narrator attempts to ground Phaedrus's theories and place the notion of Quality within the context of art, religion, and science. When Chris and his father reach the bottom of the mountain, they find other campers who offer them a ride into Bozeman, where they get a hotel room for the night.

CHAPTER TWENTY-TWO

After saying good-bye to the DeWeeses, Chris and his father head west. The narrator discusses the intersection of Phaedrus's philosophy with that of another philosopher, Jules Henri Poincaré. Near

Missoula, Montana, Chris and his father stop and eat and later find a place to camp.

CHAPTER TWENTY-THREE

This brief chapter is from Phaedrus's point of view. In the twenty-fifth anniversary edition of the book, all that is from Phaedrus's point of view is set in a font different from that of the rest of the book, to set it apart. Phaedrus recounts the dream the narrator had earlier in the book. In this version, Phaedrus understands that he is dead, and that Chris and Chris's mother and brother have come to pay their respects. Chris motions for Phaedrus to open the door, but when Phaedrus tries, a dark, shadowy figure moves between him and the door. He shouts to Chris, telling him he will see him at the bottom of the ocean because the mountain is gone.

CHAPTER TWENTY-FOUR

Waking up in Idaho, the narrator recalls the dream. Hewakes Chris and the two head out, and he is eager to begin his Chautauqua. He explores the relationship between care and Quality, pointing out that someone who recognizes Quality, and is able to experience it when he works is someone who cares. The narrator then talks about obstacles to experiencing Quality, obstacles such as one's reaction to getting stuck in any particular activity, such as motorcycle repair.

CHAPTER TWENTY-FIVE

Riding through Idaho, the narrator now discusses the "ugliness of technology" that "traditional reason" has created. He advocates viewing technology as a union of the human and the natural into a new transcendent creation, and emphasizes that the transcendence one can experience is not particular to what can be achieved through motorcycle maintenance. He goes on to discuss inner peace of mind and the way it can be achieved in various levels of understanding. They arrive in western Idaho in a town called Cambridge and camp for the night.

CHAPTER TWENTY-SIX

Chris and his father arrive in Oregon. The narrator's Chautauqua focuses on a state of being that leaves one open to Quality, and that is having gumption. The obstacle to enthusiasm is identified as "the internal gumption trap of ego," which the narrator explores with respect to motorcycle maintenance. After a lengthy discussion, the narrator points out that in reality, the metaphorical cycle he is speaking of is one's self. Chris and the narrator arrive at the West Coast and settle in for another night of camping after a long day of travel.

Part Four

CHAPTER TWENTY-SEVEN

This brief chapter opens with a dream, from Phaedrus's point of view. Phaedrus is attempting to attack the shadowy figure that comes between him and the door, him and Chris. Chris, frightened, wakes his father, who has been shouting. The narrator realizes that the person in the dream, the dreamer, is Phaedrus, and that he is the person in the shadows. He acknowledges to himself that Phaedrus is returning and that he must prepare Chris for this.

CHAPTER TWENTY-EIGHT

The narrator recalls being Phaedrus and driving with a young Chris in the car and not remembering where he was going or how to navigate in his surroundings at all. He fears endangering Chris again now. The narrator begins to recount Phaedrus's end, which began when he sought to explore Quality further in his graduate studies at the University of Chicago. While the narrator repeatedly turns to these thoughts, he and Chris arrive at Crater Lake National Park in Oregon. The narrator describes his classroom experiences in the philosophy courses in Chicago, challenging experiences with professors whose attitudes and beliefs incensed Phaedrus and drove him to further hone his understanding of Quality.

CHAPTER TWENTY-NINE

Chris, under his father's instruction, washes their clothes at the laundromat while the narrator repairs the motorcycle. His thoughts return to Quality, to his own individual view of it, and to Phaedrus's, which was larger and broader in scope. Detailed analyses of Phaedrus's clash with his professors regarding the thinking of ancient philosophers, including Aristotle, are provided by the narrator, who also pauses to note the progress of their journey into California. The narrator discusses Phaedrus's comparison of Plato's notion of the Good with his own view of Quality.

CHAPTER THIRTY

In the opening paragraph of this chapter the narrator promises to finish Phaedrus's story once and for all. He speaks of Phaedrus reading one of Plato's dialogues, the one featuring the character of Phaedrus. The solitude and aggression of the character appeal to Phaedrus. An account of the classroom discussion on the topic is presented. Phaedrus becomes increasingly withdrawn, no longer motivated to teach or to learn. He begins to feel that the more he desires to understand Quality, the more he attempts to define it, and Quality is defeated. He stops wandering and returns to his apartment, sitting cross-legged in his room for days. His consciousness dissolves; his sense of himself disintegrates. The narrator and Chris find a hotel for the night and Chris questions his father about where they are going and why he does nothing. Chris cries, rocking himself in the fetal position, claiming that he has lost an interest in wanting anything. The narrator is certain that Chris's main problem is that he misses Phaedrus.

CHAPTER THIRTY-ONE

Chris and his father leave the hotel and have breakfast. Chris expresses his desire to turn around and go home. The narrator insists that they will be heading south instead, and Chris begrudgingly climbs on the motorcycle behind his father. The narrator feels that Chris understands that his real father is no longer there. He states his feelings of having conformed. He attempts to persuade Chris to return home on a bus, and tells him he was insane for a long while, and is perhaps still insane. When Chris does not respond, the narrator also tells him of the possibility that he, Chris, may also suffer from some sort of mental illness. Chris, stunned as the import of what his father is saying sinks in, falls to the ground, rocking back and forth. A truck is approaching them, the narrator can hear it, and they are in its path. He cannot get Chris to move. When he next speaks, he recognizes the voice as not his own but Phaedrus's. It is the return of Phaedrus that prompts Chris to save his own life. Chris asks Phaedrus why he left, and if he was really insane. Phaedrus responds that they would not let him leave the hospital, and that no, he was not insane.

CHAPTER THIRTY-TWO

Chris and Phaedrus ride without helmets for the first time in the story. They can hear each other better now, and Phaedrus notes that they are connected in ways they do not even understand. Phaedrus concludes the story by stating his belief that things will be better now.

Jack Barsness

Jack Barsness and his wife Wylla visit the DeWeeses on the evening of the same day that the narrator, Chris, and the Sutherlands arrive. The narrator seems to recall that Barsness is a writer and English instructor at the University (where Phaedrus taught). An unnamed sculptor arrives at the DeWeeses after the Barsnesses appear.

Wylla Barsness

Wylla Barsness is the wife of English instructor Jack Barsness. The couple visits the DeWeeses the evening of the arrival of the narrator, Chris, and the Sutherlands.

Chris

Chris is the eleven-year-old son of the narrator. During the motorcycle trip, Chris is at times enthusiastic and happy, at other times angry; the narrator presumes these moods correspond with Chris's interpretations of and responses to his own feelings. Chris periodically complains of stomach pains, which the narrator informs the Sutherlands have no physical source but have been diagnosed as a possible symptom of mental illness. On a number of occasions throughout the journey, Chris tells his father of things his father said in his sleep and of conversations the narrator cannot recall the next day. The narrator suspects that Chris prefers his old personality of Phaedrus to his current self and begins to understand that Phaedrus is reemerging and trying to talk to Chris. At the novel's end, the narrator explains his former existence as one of insanity and tells Chris that the insanity is returning. He also tells Chris that he might have a similar mental illness. The narrator suggests that Chris return home alone. At this suggestion and upon hearing his father's description of his past life as "insane," Chris experiences a breakdown of sorts, collapsing in the road. As the narrator tries to coax him back to reality, Phaedrus emerges and speaks to Chris directly, telling him that they can at last be together. Chris's response is overwhelmingly joyful. When Chris tells Phaedrus that for all these years, he thought Phaedrus did not want to see him, Phaedrus responds that he had to do what he was told and that he was not allowed to return to his family. The narrator begins now to understand the problems Chris has had for so many years and comprehends the terror he has seen in Chris's eyes. Phaedrus now insists that he was not insane. Chris replies, "I *knew* it." In the final chapter, Chris and his father ride with their helmets off, and Chris stands behind his father to see over his head and shoulders, explaining his new perspective, saying that everything is now different. Not only has his perspective on the motorcycle changed, but his perspective on his father has as well.

Chris's Father

See Narrator

Gennie DeWeese

Gennie DeWeese and her husband host the narrator, Chris, and the Sutherlands at their Bozeman, Montana, home. The narrator confides to the DeWeeses that he is considering writing a series of essays on the philosophy of the ancient Greek rhetoricians that Plato "vilified." He describes his notion of the "Church of Reason" (the analytic reasoning taught at the University, which is mistakenly believed to encompass the whole of human understanding) to the DeWeeses. Gennie encourages the narrator in his plan to write the essays and tells him he should not worry about "trying to get it perfect."

Robert DeWeese

DeWeese is an abstract impressionist painter and an instructor of fine art at the University in Bozeman, Montana, where Phaedrus taught. The narrator, Chris, and the Sutherlands spend several nights at his house. DeWeese knew the narrator only when the narrator was in his Phaedrus phase, and the narrator is anxious about meeting DeWeese again, because he realizes that DeWeese will see him as his former personality. The narrator recalls that Phaedrus regarded DeWeese asa man with a wealth of untapped knowledge and understanding.

When the narrator, Chris, and the Sutherlands arrive at the DeWeese home, DeWeese introduces them to his other guests, an unnamed art instructor and his wife.

Narrator

The narrator of the novel is Chris's father. Years prior to the motorcycle trip, the narrator was a college instructor of rhetoric. He was a gifted child with a high IQ who entered college at the age of fifteen and was expelled two years later. He served in the army, in Korea, and returned to complete his education. After he began teaching in Bozeman, Montana, he pondered the philosophical questions he was so plagued by in his earlier years. Gradually he became obsessed with the metaphysical notion of Quality and its role as an organizing principle in the universe. Unable to find a way to incorporate his philosophy into his everyday life, he became increasingly withdrawn and isolated, a stranger to his family and friends. He was committed to a mental institution, diagnosed with schizophrenia, and treated with electro-shock therapy. When he returned to society, he had what his doctors described as a new and different personality. The narrator comes to view his old self as another identity entirely and names him Phaedrus, after a character in one of the Greek philosopher Plato's dialogues. The new personality —the narrator—is not identified by name. His son calls him Dad, and the other characters in the book never refer to him by name. References to emptiness and loneliness in the novel suggest that he feels cut off, isolated from his true self. He seems to want to put Phaedrus behind him for good, to "bury" him, yet he seems to be running toward Phaedrus at the same time, returning to his college office and classroom and following his route across the country and through the mountains. Throughout the novel, the narrator accesses more and more of the remnants of Phaedrus's thought and follows the philosophical paths created by Phaedrus to new directions that Phaedrus had not pursued. When the narrator understands at last, after a series of dreams, that Phaedrus is reemerging, he attempts to prepare Chris. He draws out the journey in order to spend more time with Chris and then tells his son some of the truth about his past, saying that he wants to send Chris home alone. Chris is unable to bear this news. The breakdown that follows draws Phaedrus out and reunites father and son. In the final chapter of the book, the narrator/Phaedrus concludes his narration with a declaration of victory. "We've won it," he says. "It's going to get better now."

Phaedrus

See Narrator

Sarah

Sarah is a woman the narrator recalls after he enters his old office at the college in Bozeman, Montana. Her office was adjacent to Phaedrus's, and it was her statement to him, "I hope you are teaching Quality to your students," that set Phaedrus on his obsessive quest for an understanding of Quality.

John Sutherland

John Sutherland and his wife, Sylvia, are friends of the narrator. They accompany the narrator and his son Chris on the motorcycle trip from Minnesota to Montana. While the couple provides amiable company for the narrator throughout much of the journey, the narrator also identifies areas in which his and John's approaches to motorcycles, and to life, are in opposition to one another. Due to this difference, John is used by the narrator as an example of the romantic, intuitive, anti-technological mindset as opposed to the classic, reasoning, technological one. Despite the deep differences in the philosophies of John and the narrator, the narrator observes that John is worth the effort of reasoning with and of trying to understand. The narrator also informs the reader that he and the Sutherlands have been on a number of motorcycle trips together in the past and that John is a musician.

Sylvia Sutherland

Sylvia Sutherland and her husband John are friends of the narrator who travel with him for some of the journey. She is depicted as contemplative, amiable, and pleasant, and in complete agreement with her husband in terms of their romantic approach to life, an approach that is disdainful of technology, according to the narrator. Sylvia expresses both concern about Chris and his stomach pains and occasional annoyance with Chris's behavior.

Classicism versus Romanticism

In *Zen and the Art of Motorcycle Maintenance*, the narrator discusses two schools of thought—classicism and romanticism—and explores the reasons these branches of thinking have been set in opposition to one another throughout history. He advocates for a unification of these two ways of approaching the world, stating that "classic and romantic understanding should be united at a basic level." The narrator also explains that Phaedrus's quest was to solve this philosophical dilemma. The classical school of thought or mode of thinking, as the narrator describes it, is associated with analysis, reasoning, science, technology, and technological methods. Romanticism is associated with art, intuition, and the view that technology is ugly. The Sutherlands are identified by the narrator as representatives of romanticism. Throughout the novel, the narrator offers examples of the ways these two modes of thought are viewed in terms of their opposition to one another. He speaks of the way abstract art is derided by the scientifically minded and how technical tasks such as motorcycle repair are feared by individuals with a more intuitive mind-set. He explains that romantics see things for what they are, appreciating the beauty of the object as it is, while classicists see things for what they do, appreciating the function of each component.

When the narrator is asked by Robert DeWeese to examine the instructions for putting together a rotisserie, the discussion arises again. DeWeese, an artist, is unable to make sense of the technical assembly instructions. The narrator claims that the reason for this is at least in part because the instructions were written without an appreciation for the rotisserie as a whole. The instruction writer focused on the pieces, while DeWeese focused on his desire for the completed whole. This points to the disconnection and resulting isolation the narrator spends much of the book discussing. Had the instruction writer appreciated the various ways the parts could be assembled to make a functioning unit, and had DeWeese had that same appreciation, rather than the impatience for only the end result, there would likely not have been a problem. As the narrator points out, "This divorce of art from technology is completely unnatural."

Metaphysical Quality

The narrator's gradual solution to the divorce of art and technology is the idea of Quality. Phaedrus arrives at a philosophical, metaphysical idea of Quality. (Metaphysics is a branch of philosophy dealing with the principles of reality and nature of being, as well as an exploration of concepts which the sciences accept as fact.) The notion of Quality, or Quality in the metaphysical way Phaedrus considers it, is his solution to the classic versus romantic split. He sees the notion of Quality as a "new spiritual *rationality*—in which the ugliness and the loneliness and the spiritual blankness" provided by traditional classic versus romantic thinking "would become illogical."

The narrator, however, takes a different approach, focusing instead on attitudes, making Quality "occur at the individual level, on a personal basis, in one's own life, in a less dramatic way." The ideas of care and of gumption are the more practical approaches to experiencing Quality advocated by the narrator. Phaedrus and the narrator offer different details and structures to support their theories about Quality. For Phaedrus, the details include analyses of the philosophies of Immanuel Kant, David Hume, Aristotle, and Plato. He offers a reasoned approach to the existence of Quality despite its inability to be defined. As an instructor at the University, he proved that his students could identify Quality (in the writing of other students), even though they could not explain or define it. The narrator offers instead details regarding the specific features of various motorcycle repair jobs. He discusses a variety of parts, their functions, and the way to avoid a "gumption trap" like anxiety or ego, traps which inhibit Quality. He discusses "stuckness" and the meditative way this state can be approached in order to yield a more enlightened understanding of the motorcycle as a fusion of both art and technology.

Topics for Further Study

- Some critics have compared *Zen and the Art of Motorcycle Maintenance* to the 1851 novel *Moby Dick* by Herman Melville. On the surface, these books seem very different, one centering on a cross-country motorcycle trip, the other set at sea and focusing on a whale hunt. Yet both the narrator of *Zen and the Art of Motorcycle Maintenance* and Ishmael of *Moby Dick* deal with issues of personal identity while exploring the nature of the universe and their places in it. Read *Moby Dick*. What themes does it share with *Zen and the Art of Motorcycle Maintenance*? How are the main characters and their concerns alike? How are they different? Compare the endings of the novels. How do the resolutions differ? What is the fate of the main characters? Write an essay on your findings.

- The motorcycle journey taken in *Zen and the Art of Motorcycle Maintenance* has become a popular route for motorcycle enthusiasts and fans of the novel. Using the book as your guide, plot the route taken first by Chris, his father, and the Sutherlands, and later by just Chris and his father. Create a Web page or PowerPoint presentation that maps their route and the stops the travelers made along the way.

- In *Zen and the Art of Motorcycle Maintenance*, the narrator has a history of mental illness, and he suggests that his son might also suffer from some degree of mental illness. Chris's stomach aches, we are told, are a symptom of such problems. Using both Internet and print sources, research schizophrenia, the mental illness with which the narrator was diagnosed. Study the ways in which such a diagnosis was treated during the 1950s and compare these methods, which the novel informs us included electro-shock therapy, with modern methods of treatment. Create a PowerPoint or similar visual presentation in which you present the findings of your research. Be sure to include the proper documentation of your Internet and print sources.

- The young-adult novel *The Absolutely True Diary of a Part-Time Indian*, by Sherman Alexie, published in 2009 by Little, Brown Young Readers, is like *Zen and the Art of Motorcycle Maintenance* in that it is a semi-autobiographical work in which the narrator explores questions of his own identity and his identity within a larger community. Read Alexie's novel and compare its main character (Arnold Spirit) to both the narrator of *Zen and the Art of Motorcycle Maintenance* and to the narrator's son, Chris. In what ways are the characters' concerns about their personal identities similar? Note their similar senses of isolation and consider reasons for this common feeling. To what extent are Arnold Spirit's experiences of isolation generated by his racial identity? Prepare an oral or written report in which you compare the characters in these works.

- In *Zen and the Art of Motorcycle Maintenance*, the character of Chris is seen only from the eyes of his troubled father. We see the narrator's concern for Chris and understand at the novel's end how much the narrator believes Chris has helped him along his journey. Rewrite the ending of the book from Chris's point of view. Reflect on the whole journey up to this point from Chris's perspective. Examine the novel for clues regarding Chris's perceptions of his father. When does he fear him? When does he feel a sense of connection? How do experiences early on in the journey affect the events of the last three chapters?

The two take different approaches to the same goal. Phaedrus eventually comes to recognize Quality as the same concept as the Tao, the "Way," as explored in the *Tao Te Ching* by Lao Tzu. (Taoism is a Chinese philosophy that focuses on achieving a spiritual harmony with nature.) The narrator comes to identify his meditative approach to his motorcycle and his life with the Zen Buddhist tradition. (Zen Buddhism is a Japanese philosophy advocating meditation as a path toward spiritual enlightenment.)

First-Person Narrative

Zen and the Art of Motorcycle Maintenance is written as a first-person narrative describing the cross-country motorcycle trip of the narrator and his companions. The unnamed narrator refers to himself as "I." The sections of the book in which the account of the narrator's travels with his son are being directly related are written in present tense, as are the narrator's thoughts on motorcycle maintenance and his personal thoughts on the larger implications of motorcycle maintenance attitudes. The narrator's recollections of Phaedrus and the explanation of Phaedrus's thoughts are written in past tense, as this personality, his thoughts, and the events of his life occurred in the narrator's past.

In any first-person narrative, the reliability of the narrator is a subject for consideration: the reader has only the narrator's account of events as a guide. As this particular story unfolds, the reader realizes that the narrator has a history of mental illness, thereby calling into question the accuracy of all of his observations and thoughts. Yet the narrator of *Zen and the Art of Motorcycle Maintenance*, through both his awareness of his past mental illness and his calm, intellectual, and intelligent way of interacting and expressing himself, establishes a sense of trustworthiness. This view of the narrator as reliable is undercut by the existence of verbal exchanges with his son that he cannot recall, and readers are left to resolve this issue on their own, weighing his apparent intelligence and normalcy against his history of mental illness and the resurgence of his former personality. Readers must also ask whether or not his past or current insanity actually inhibits his ability to be trustworthy and reliable as a narrator.

Extended Metaphor

Throughout the novel, Pirsig uses motorcycle maintenance as a metaphor for the maintenance of the spiritual/philosophical well-being of an individual. A metaphor is a figure of speech in which two different objects or concepts are equated to one another. Pirsig, for example, early on in the narrator's journey, uses an oncoming storm as a metaphor for the emotional conflict the narrator is approaching.

A person would not normally refer to caring for himself as motorcycle maintenance. But Pirsig applies his ideas about a person's attitudes toward motorcycle maintenance to his attitudes about his spiritual and philosophical world view. Because he does this throughout the course of the novel, repeatedly drawing the reader's attention to these parallels, the metaphor is referred to as an extended metaphor. Pirsig directly addresses this relationship (between motorcycle maintenance attitudes and personal/spiritual/philosophical attitudes) when the narrator observes that

> the real cycle you're working on is a
> cycle called yourself. The machine
> that appears to be "out there" and the
> person that appears to be "in here"
> are not two separate things. They
> grow toward Quality or fall away
> from Quality together.

The narrator advocates looking at life in the
same way that one looks at motorcycle maintenance
—seeing the fusion of art and technology in all of
humanity, approaching tasks with care, and
focusing on the task itself without rushing or
wishing to get to the final product or the next
destination faster. At the novel's end, Chris asks
about having a motorcycle when he is older. His
father tells him he may have one, if he takes care of
it. The narrator tells Chris that it is not difficult to
properly care for a motorcycle "if you have the right
attitudes. It's having the right attitudes that's hard."
What these right attitudes are is what he has been
explaining throughout the novel; his discussion of
motorcycle maintenance dovetails with his thoughts
on the integration and the transcendence of art and
technology.

The extended metaphor of motorcycle
maintenance provides overarching structure to the
novel. In addition, Pirsig makes use of metaphorical
language throughout the book. For example, the
narrator's comparison of his former personality,
Phaedrus, to a ghost, is another use of metaphor.
This comparison encourages the readers to think

that Phaedrus is dead and that his memory haunts the narrator in powerful ways. Similarly, the journey the narrator and his son take up the mountain serves as a metaphor for the narrator's journey toward a greater understanding of Phaedrus, toward his ultimate enlightenment. Significantly, the narrator refuses to reach the summit of the mountain, turning to make the descent before the full completion of the journey, much to his son's disappointment. He is not yet ready to completely face Phaedrus, and the failure to reach the summit is noted by Chris when he accuses his father of not being brave.

Conservative Reactions to Communist Fears in the 1950s

Zen and the Art of Motorcycle Maintenance was published in 1974, but it takes place in two different time periods. The Phaedrus phase of the narrator's life occurs in the 1950s. The real-life motorcycle trip Pirsig writes about in the novel took place in 1968, several years prior to the book's publication, but within the same general cultural atmosphere. The narrator relates a few things about both time periods. In Montana in the late 1950s, the place and time in which Phaedrus taught there, was what the narrator describes as "an outbreak of ultra-rightwing politics." Through his narrator, Pirsig highlights some of the conservative policies of the University administration. He relates that the public statements of professors had to be approved by the administration, and the academic standards of the college were, in Phaedrus's opinion, deteriorating in order to increase enrollment. The University's accreditation status would be affected unless the broad enrollment guidelines were enforced.

Compare & Contrast

- **1950s:** The United States is involved in a war against Communist aggression in Korea. Pirsig writes about serving in Korea (prior to the Korean War) in *Zen and the Art of Motorcycle Maintenance* and also about the conservative, anti-Communist attitudes pervasive in the United States at the time.

1970s: The spread of Communism is now being fought, with the aid of the United States, in Vietnam. A cultural battle between conservatives who feel that Communism is a world-wide threat and anti-war liberals pervades the country. The opposing value systems at war are reflective of the classic/romantic divide Pirsig explores in his novel.

Today: The United States is involved in a lengthy war in Iraq, a war which originally saw a considerable amount of popular support. This support has waned as the United States involvement has continued, and distrust toward people of Arab descent is not uncommon.

- **1950s:** There is a great deal of social stigma attached to mental illness, particularly forms more severe than anxiety or depression, such as the narrator's diagnosed schizophrenia in *Zen and the Art of Motorcycle*

Maintenance. Society is, in general, intolerant of nonconformity.

1970s: While there remains some stigma attached to mental illness, societal attitudes are less judgmental than in the 1950s. There is a trend toward deinstitutionalizing individuals who had previously been committed for various forms of mental illness, inspired in part by the desire of mental health professionals hoping to break the social stigma of mental illness. Yet, many individuals suffer as a result of the loss of proper care and treatment.

Today: The social stigma surrounding mental illness persists. Even individuals who receive proper care are sometimes denied employment. Social fears regarding the possible violent tendencies of individuals suffering from mental illness have increased since the 1950s. Despite the plethora of new medications designed to treat various mental illness, many individuals diagnosed with mental illness are not properly treated.

- **1950s:** In 1957, Jack Kerouac's *On the Road* is published by Viking Press. The work ushers in the modern road trip novel as an immensely popular genre. Kerouac's fictionalized autobiography receives immediate critical acclaim as well as popular success.

1970s: The road trip genre thrives. In 1974, Pirsig's road trip novel, *Zen and the Art of Motorcycle Maintenance*, is beloved by many not only for its philosophical commentary but also for its beautifully written account of the motorcycle trip from Minnesota to California, a route fans of the book have followed religiously since the novel's publication. Like Kerouac's novel, Pirsig's book is a somewhat fictionalized account of his real-life experiences.

Today: As a genre, the road trip novel remains appealing and successful. Modern examples of the genre include literary novels, such as *Ash Wednesday*, written by actor-director Ethan Hawke and published by Vintage in 2003, and young-adult fiction, such as the novel *Shift*, by Jennifer Bradbury, which features an account of a bicycle road trip taken by teens.

Phaedrus objected to this policy. The Montana

State University Web site confirms that the expansion of the school was brought about by a lowering of academic standards, which the president of the university allowed but with which he apparently did not agree. According to Montana State University, the president (Roland Renne) was "forced to downplay his ideals in order to secure funds for the expansion" of the school.

While the narrator focuses on Phaedrus's particular concerns about the school's accreditation, the university's Web site also confirms the truth about a general atmosphere of fear and resulting conservatism and names the fear of Communism that began to seep across the country as a cause. Such heightened concern about Communism was generated in part by the Korean War and by McCarthyism and the Red Scare. The United States's involvement in the Korean War took place from 1950 to 1953 and was centered around the U.S. defense of South Korea against Communist North Korea. Fear of the spread of Communism became pervasive in the United States, as the Communist Union of Soviet Socialist Republics (U.S.S.R.) was becomingly increasingly powerful. Senator Joseph McCarthy was famous for claiming to have a list of accused Communists who worked for the U.S. State Department. His accusations were unproven, but he gained national support for his interest in finding and convicting suspected communists of treason.

Social Activism in the Late 1960s

and Early 1970s

Whereas Pirsig, in his novel, offers specifics regarding the conservative atmosphere of the university setting in the 1950s, his portrayal of the cultural atmosphere of the late 1960s and early 1970s is more vague. And for neither time frame does he discuss national political events, such as the Korean War or the Vietnam War. He mentions that Phaedrus served in Korea, but the context provided, along with known biographical facts of Pirsig's life, shows that his service was prior to the war. With regard to the late 1960s and early 1970s, Pirsig's novel paints a picture of what is wrong with society in terms of general, negative reactions to technology. Pervading the novel is the idea that because so many people view the world in terms of the classic/romantic split, everyone suffers from the tension created. He speaks of the need to reform attitudes.

This desire for societal reformation, the narrator insists, must be accomplished on a personal level before society can change, but the desire itself for inner peace and the longing to "reform the world, and make it a better place to live in," are reflective of the activism of the time period. The United States's involvement in the Vietnam War (1959-1975) was lengthy, and as U.S. military presence there grew, so did the opposition to it back in the United States. During the late 1950s, the most pervasive fear in the United States was the fear of communism. In the late 1960s and early 1970s, the deeper fear seems to have been with the way the

United States was fighting the war against the spread of communism. War protesters learned from the activism of the everyday citizens involved in the civil rights movement, citizens who were successful in making changes to government policies. Both the civil rights and the anti-war movements focused on peaceful activities for advocating change: they staged marches, rallies, and parades; they spread their message through speeches and publications; and they petitioned the government for change.

The narrator directly contrasts the conservatism of the 1950s with the liberalism of the 1970s by stating, "This was the nineteen-fifties, not the nineteen-seventies. There were rumblings from the beatniks and early hippies at this time about 'the system' and the square intellectualism that supported it, but hardly anyone guessed how deeply the whole edifice would be brought into doubt."

Critical Overview

Criticism of *Zen and the Art of Motorcycle Maintenance* tends to combine analysis of the work as a literary endeavor and as a philosophical treatise. Some earlier reviewers were quick to recognize the dual nature of the book. W. T. Lhamon, for example, in a 1974 review in the *New Republic*, observes the sluggish way the book, encumbered with its philosophical baggage, plods along, but comes together at the end. Lhamon praises the novel's way of tackling the big ideas of nature and technology, comparing Pirsig to Melville and, ironically, Thoreau, whom the narrator of *Zen and the Art of Motorcycle Maintenance* criticizes. The reviewer predicts, "There will be a lot of people reading this novel and it may well become an American classic." Likewise, Robert M. Adams, in a 1974 review appearing in the *New York Review of Books*, comments on the somewhat clunky way the story progresses. Yet Adams also praises Pirsig's rich prose, maintaining that even if the novel's "confused metaphysics" should fade, the novel's "wonder and fear" would persist. The book's dualities, it's attempt to balance the narrative regarding father and son with the philosophical doctrines of Phaedrus, were also noted by critic George Steiner. In his 1974 review for the *New Yorker*, he finds much to praise about Pirsig's novel, which he considers perhaps intentionally awkward.

In Una Allis's 1978 article for *Critical*

Quarterly, the critic observes the warm critical and popular reception *Zen and the Art of Motorcycle Maintenance* received. Allis goes on to review the novel's philosophical content, and to assess it in terms of its realism. Taking another approach to understanding the novel, Richard H. Rodino, in a 1980 article for *Critique: Studies in Modern Fiction*, examines the irony inherent in the relationship between the novel's action and the commentary of the narrator. Rodino finds that in studying the instances of such irony, the reader must balance his understanding of what the novel seems to be teaching with the knowledge of the novel's warning regarding the "dangers of being taught." This practice, Rodino insists, reveals "new discoveries" that the reader makes alongside the narrator.

The narrator's insistence on the integration of art and technology, and his views on the split between the romantic and classic modes of thinking, have been explored by those in technical fields. In a 1975 article for *Science*, George Basalla assures readers that Pirsig's novel does not attack the fields of science and technology. Basalla explores the ways in which the narrator and Phaedrus seek unification, rather than preaching further division. James Willis writes in an article in a 2000 edition of *Journal of Medical Ethics*, "In the seventies it would have been thought madness to suggest that medical practice could be defined by rigid rules. Today it is our tragedy to live at a time when this bizarre idea is orthodoxy." Similarly, in a 1994 article in *Technical Communication*, Charles Beck examines Pirsig's use of "the rhetoric of technical communication" to study the finer points of the classic/romantic divide.

What Do I Read Next?

- Pirsig's sequel to *Zen and the Art of Motorcycle Maintenance* is *Lila: An Inquiry Into Morals* (published by Bantam in 1991). In this second novel, Pirsig continues the story of Phaedrus, who is now traveling the Hudson River by boat when he meets Lila, a woman with mental instabilities of her own. Phaedrus's relationship with Lila leads to insights that enable him to further shape his theory of Quality.

- *Zen and Now: On the Trail of Robert Pirsig and the Art of Motorcycle Maintenance*, by Mark

Richardson, published by Knopf in 2008, is an exploration of Pirsig's life and his philosophy as expressed in *Zen and the Art of Motorcycle Maintenance*. It is also a travelogue of Richardson's motorcycle trek along Pirsig's former route from Minnesota to California, as Pirsig detailed the journey in his novel.

- *Zen Mind, Beginner's Mind*, by Shunryu Suzuki, published by Shambala in 2006, is a collection of excerpts from Suzuki's lectures on Zen Buddhism, presented with the beginner American Buddhist in mind. As an introduction to Buddhism for an American audience, the book helps explain the belief system Pirsig embraces in his novel.

- *Picture Perfect* is a young adult novel by Elaine Marie Alphin, published in 2003 by First Avenue Editions. A first-person narrative, the book is a psychological mystery in which the reader is exposed to three distinct personalities of the narrator. It offers an exploration of psychological issues similar to those examined in *Zen and the Art of Motorcycle Maintenance*, but is told from the perspective of a teenage boy.

- *Let Their Spirits Dance* by Stella Pope Duarte is, like *Zen and the Art of Motorcycle Maintenance*, a novel that utilizes the road trip format as a metaphor for the journey of confronting the past. It concerns a Hispanic American family and their grief over a family member who died serving in the Vietnam War. The book was published in 2003 by Harper Perennial.

- Actors Ewan McGregor and Charley Boorman, both motorcycle aficionados, realized it was possible to ride all the way around the world if they could be transported across the Bering Strait. Though their journey was possible, it was not without difficulties, and their resulting journey of over 20,000 miles in four months was recorded in *Long Way Round: Chasing Shadows across the World* (published by Atria in 2004). The memoir, like *Zen and the Art of Motorcycle Maintenance*, includes retellings of the adventures and introspections of the two actors as they found their lives changed by the experience.

Sources

Adams, Robert M., "Good Trip," in *Guidebook to Zen and the Art of Motorcycle Maintenance*, by Robert L. DiSanto and Thomas J. Steele, William Morrow, 1990, pp. 240-337; originally published in *New York Review of Books*, June 13, 1974, pp. 22-23.

Adams, Tim, "The Interview: Robert Pirsig," in the *Observer*, November 19, 2006, Features Section, p. 4.

Allis, Una, "Zen and the Art of Motorcycle Maintenance," in *Critical Quarterly*, Vol. 20, No. 3, September 1978, pp. 33-41.

"Anti-Vietnam War Movement," in *MSN Encarta*, http://encarta.msn.com/encyclopedia_761589794/Ar Vietnam_War_Movement.html (accessed May 1, 2009).

Basalla, George, "Man and Machine," in *Science*, Vol. 187, No. 4173, January 24, 1975, pp. 248-50.

Beck, Charles E., "The Most Famous Yet Unusual Technical Writer (Technical Writer Robert Pirsig)," in *Technical Communication*, Vol. 41, No. 2, May 1994, pp. 354-58.

Borinstein, Andrew B., "Public Attitudes toward Persons with Mental Illness," *Health Affairs*, Fall 1992, pp. 186-96.

Bump, Jerome, "Creativity, Rationality, and

Metaphor in Robert Pirsig's *Zen and the Art of Motorcycle Maintenance*," in *South Atlantic Quarterly*, Vol. 82, No. 4, 1983, pp. 370-80.

Byrne, Peter, "Zen Rides Again: Robert Pirsig's *Zen and the Art of Motorcycle Maintenance*," in *Swans Commentary*, August 11, 2008, http://www.swans.com/library/art14/pbyrne78.html (accessed May 6, 2009).

"Chapter 1: Introduction and Themes," in *Mental Health: A Report of the Surgeon General*, United States Office of the Surgeon General Web site, http://www.surgeongeneral.gov/library/mentalhealth (accessed May 6, 2009).

DiSanto, Ronald L. and Thomas J. Steele, "A Philosophical Backpack—Eastern Philosophy," and "A Philosophical Backpack—Western Philosophy," in *Guidebook to Zen and the Art of Motorcycle Maintenance*, William Morrow and Company, 1990, pp. 50-133, 134-204.

Lhamon, W. T., "A Fine Fiction," in the *New Republic*, Vol. 170, June 29, 1974, pp. 24-26.

"Montana State University History: 1950-1959," in *Montana State University* Web site, http://www.montana.edu/msuhistory/1950.html (accessed May 1, 2009).

Pirsig, Robert M., *Zen and the Art of Motorcycle Maintenance: An Inquiry into Values*, Perennial Classics, 2000.

Rodino, Richard H., "Irony and Earnestness in Robert Pirsig's *Zen and the Art of Motorcycle*

Maintenance," in *Guidebook to Zen and the Art of Motorcycle Maintenance*, by Robert L. DiSanto and Thomas J. Steele, William Morrow, 1990, pp. 240-337; originally published in *Critique: Studies in Modern Fiction*, Vol. 22, 1980, pp. 21-31.

"Role of Deinstitutionalization" and "Inadequacies with the Current Mental Health System," in *Mental Health Association of Westchester* Web site, http://www.mhawestchester.org/advocates/agendao2 (accessed May 6, 2009).

Steiner, George, "Uneasy Rider," in the *New Yorker*, April 15, 1974, pp. 147-50.

"Timeline: Iraq After Saddam," *BBC News*, http://news.bbc.co.uk/2/hi/middle_east/4192189.stm (accessed May 5, 2009).

"United States History: The Korean War, "*MSN Encarta*, http://encarta.msn.com/encyclopedia_1741500823_2 (accessed May, 1, 2009).

Willis, James, "A Personal Response to *Zen and the Art of Motorcycle Maintenance*," in *Journal of Medical Ethics*, Vol. 26, No. 6, December 2000, p. 110.

Further Reading

Garripoli, Garri, *The Tao of the Ride: Motorcycles and the Mechanics of the Soul*, HCI, 1999.

> Garripoli's work is a nonfiction exploration of the relationship between Eastern philosophy and motorcycle riding. While Garripoli uses the motorcycle journey as a metaphor for the journey of life, his descriptions of the motorcycle road trip focus on the details of the actual physical trip.

Hinshaw, Stephen P., *The Mark of Shame: Stigma of Mental Illness and an Agenda for Change*, Oxford University Press, 2006.

> Hinshaw offers an analysis of the stigma attached to mental illness and studies the way societal views and judgments have changed over the last fifty years.

Hoff, Benjamin, *The Tao of Pooh*, Dutton, 1982.

> Hoff provides an accessible introduction to the Eastern philosophy known as Taoism, which Pirsig references in his novel. Phaedrus observes the parallels between his own thinking and the *Tao Te Ching*, an ancient work

composed by Lao Tzu. Hoff compares Taoism with the other Eastern philosophies of Buddhism and Confucianism, using the A. A. Milne children's book characters of Winnie the Pooh and Piglet.

Kerouac, Jack, *On the Road*, Viking, 1957.

Kerouac's novel introduced a format and narrative style that many critics believe influenced Pirsig's novel.

Larsen, Karen, *Breaking the Limit: One Woman's Motorcycle Journey through North America*, Hyperion, 2004.

Larsen offers an account of a cross-country motorcycle trip from a woman's perspective. Her work is a combination of essay and travelogue and is filled with Pirsig-like observations on the towns she stops in, the camping she does, and the road she travels.

Plato, *The Dialogues of Plato*, introduced by Erich Segal, Bantam Classic, 1986.

This collection of several of Plato's philosophical dialogues includes *Gorgias*, featuring the character of Phaedrus, after whom the narrator names his alternate personality.